我們靠自己

劉墉 —— 中文·圖
劉倚帆 —— 英文
劉軒 —— 監製

We
Rely
on
Ourselves

Yong Liu
Yvonne Liu
Xuan Liu

故事裡有故事

不久前，我出版《小沙彌遇見劉墉》，承蒙星雲大師寫序，大師在序裡說他早年剛到臺灣的時候，常常借廟口演講，發現只要他講故事，群眾就會漸漸向他集中，故事講完開始說理了，大家又慢慢散去。等他再講故事，大家又聚攏過來。一場演講大約兩個鐘頭，群眾就像潮水一樣，聚散好幾次。

我四十多年前在丹維爾作駐館藝術家的時候，也有類似的經驗：美術館為了推展中華文化，可能早上要我去教小學生，晚上又安排我在研究所演講。那時候我的英文很差，不太能說道理，只好講故事。我發現不論對小朋友或研究生，最討好的就是說故事，其中又以寓言故事為佳。因為同一個故事可以讓小孩目不轉睛，也可以讓大學生興味盎然，多年之後學生可能把我的名字都忘了，還會提起我當年講過的故事。

這本書裡就收集了我過去五十年間寫的寓言故事，有些很簡短，像是沙漠跟海洋利益交換、貓跟狗劃分地盤、魚跟鉤比賽打賭、毛蟲對上帝抱怨。有些比較寫實，像是富翁的大房簷、十二個孩子、三把麵條和傳家寶，還有些是以較長的童話故事出現，像是鞋子們開大會、老虎跟猴子吹牛、橡樹與小草對話。

　　古人談詩，說詩有一個好處是可以「主文而譎諫，言之者無罪，聞之者足以戒」，意思是透過婉轉比喻的方式勸人，可以讓被勸的人自己思考，而不至於傷面子。我的寓言故事應該也如此，小朋友可能看到的是花草蟲魚老虎貓咪，成年人卻可能咀嚼出背後反諷的東西。有趣味又能玩味的東西容易流傳，希望有一天大家雖然把我遺忘，還能記得這本書裡的一些小故事。

Stories Within Stories

Not long ago, I published *Little Monk Meets Yong Liu*, with thanks to Master Hsing Yun for writing the foreword. Master Hsing Yun wrote about when he first arrived in Taiwan. He frequently lectured at temple gates and realized that whenever he told stories, the crowds gradually gathered around him. When he finished the stories and spoke about theories, people gradually dispersed. When he told a story again, people gathered around again. Over the course of each two-hour lecture, the crowds were like tides, gathering and dispersing multiple times.

Forty years ago, when I was Artist-in-Residence at the Danville Museum, I had a similar experience. To promote Chinese culture, the art museum sometimes had me teach elementary school children in the morning and graduate school students in the evening. My English skills were poor at that time; I could not explain theories well, so I told stories. I realized that regardless of whether they were young children or graduate students, the best way to please them was by telling stories, especially fables. The same story could make children become intently focused and also make older students become enthusiastically fascinated. Many years later, there were students who probably forgot my name but still mentioned the stories I told back then.

This book compiles fables that I wrote over the past 50 years. Some are short—such as the desert and the ocean negotiating benefits, a cat and a dog setting boundaries, a fish and a hook making a bet, and a caterpillar complaining to God. Some are realistic—such as "The Rich Man's Eaves," "Twelve Children," "Three Bundles of Noodles," and "The Family Heirloom." Some are in the form of longer fairy tales—such as shoes holding a symposium, a tiger boasting to a monkey, and an oak tree conversing with grass.

When the old masters discussed poetry, they said that a benefit of poetry is how it can use tactful metaphors to persuade, so that the people being persuaded can ponder on their own without feeling humiliated. My fables should work similarly. Children might only see the flower, grass, bug, fish, tiger, cat, etc.—while adults might chew on the underlying satire. Amusing stories that can be slowly appreciated are easier to pass on. I hope that one day, when people will have forgotten me, they can still remember some stories from this book.

我們
靠自己
We Rely on
Ourselves

我們靠自己

We Rely on Ourselves

「媽媽！為什麼我從出生，就要背這個又重又硬的殼呢？真是累死了！」小蝸牛問媽媽。

「因為我們的身體沒有骨骼的支撐，只能爬，爬又爬不快。」媽媽說。

「毛蟲姐姐沒有骨頭，也爬不快，為什麼她不用背又重又硬的殼呢？」

「因為毛蟲姐姐能變成蝴蝶，天空會保護她。」

「蚯蚓弟弟沒有骨頭，也爬不快，更不會變，他為什麼不背又重又硬的殼呢？」

「因為蚯蚓弟弟會鑽土，大地會保護他。」

小蝸牛哭了起來：「我好可憐，天空不保護，大地也不保護。」

「所以我們有殼啊！」蝸牛媽媽拍拍小蝸牛 ：「我們不靠天，也不靠地，我們靠自己。」

"Mom, why do we have to carry this hard and heavy shell our whole lives? It's so exhausting!" the little snail asked its mother.

"Because we don't have a skeleton to support us. We can only crawl — slowly," Mother answered.

"Miss Caterpillar has no bones and crawls slowly too. Why doesn't she carry a hard and heavy shell?"

"Because Miss Caterpillar can turn into a butterfly. The sky will protect her."

"Mr. Earthworm has no bones, crawls slowly, and doesn't turn into anything else. Why doesn't he carry a hard and heavy shell?"

"Because Mr. Earthworm can dig into the soil. The earth will protect him."

The little snail started to cry. "Poor me! The sky doesn't protect me, and neither does the earth."

"That is why we have shells!" Mother comforted the little snail. "We do not rely on the sky, and we do not rely on the earth. We rely on ourselves."

河與橋的爭執

A Quarrel Between
the River and the Bridge

13

河跟橋不高興：「你為什麼凌駕我，讓我感覺被壓迫？而且人們總是在你上面跑來跑去，吵死了！還丟垃圾下來汙染我，髒死了！」

　　橋對河說：「問題是我從來也沒阻擋過你，只會超越你。你繼續流你的，我們互不相干。而且當你從西往東，我就從北往南；當你從北往南，我就從東往西，我從來跟你不是一個方向啊！」

　　他們的爭辯聲把岸吵醒了，揉揉眼睛說：「去！去！去！你們一個把我切開，一個把兩頭架在我身上，我都不怨，你們還怨什麼？」

The river was upset at the bridge: "Why do you override me and make me feel oppressed? Also, people are always running around on you—super noisy! They even toss down trash to pollute me—super dirty!"

The bridge said to the river, "I have never blocked you; I only surpass you. You continue to flow as you wish. We don't interfere with each other. When you go west to east, I go north to south; when you go north to south, I go east to west. I never go in the same direction as you!"

The sounds of their quarrelling woke up the riverbank. The riverbank rubbed its eyes and said, "Go away! Go away! One of you cuts me open, while the other one of you stands with both ends on my body. If I don't even complain, then what right do you have to complain?"

公平的談判

●

Fair Negotiations

一

有一天，沙漠和海洋談判。

「我太乾，乾得連一條小溪都沒有，你卻水太多，變成汪洋一片。」沙漠建議：「我們不如來個交換吧！」

「好啊！」海洋欣然同意：「我歡迎沙漠來填補海洋，但是我已經有沙灘了，所以只要土，不要沙。」

「我也歡迎海洋來滋潤沙漠。」沙漠說：「可是鹽太鹹了，所以只要水，不要鹽。」

二

　　有一天，黃狗和花貓舉行談判。

　　「土地屬於我，屋頂屬於你，我們劃清界線，誰也不侵犯誰，好不好？」黃狗說。

　　「好極了！」花貓欣然同意。

　　「我從沒上過屋頂，你卻常到地面，這是過去的事 ，我姑且原諒你。」黃狗得意地說：「但是從今以後，我不上你的屋頂，你也不准到地面來，否則你違約，我就要對你不客氣了！」

◉

　　有的談判看來很理想，卻永遠談不成。
　　有的談判看來很公平，卻有人吃大虧。

One

One day, the desert negotiated with the ocean.

"I'm parched, with nary a stream. Meanwhile, you have too much water—nothing but water for miles. Why don't we trade!" the desert suggested.

"Sounds good!" the ocean gladly agreed. "I welcome the desert to create land in the ocean, but I already have beaches. So, I only want soil—no sand please."

"I also welcome the ocean to hydrate the desert lands," the desert said, "but salt is too salty. So, I only want freshwater— no salt please."

Two

One day, a dog negotiated with a cat.

"The ground belongs to me, and the roof belongs to you. Let's make that clear and not encroach on each other. What do you say?" the dog said.

"Fantastic!" the cat gladly agreed.

"I have never been on the roof, yet you are often on the ground. But we can let bygones be bygones. I'll forgive you," the dog said proudly. "However, from now on, I won't go to the roof, and you better not come to the ground. Don't violate our agreement, or else I won't be nice anymore!"

◉

Some negotiations seem ideal, but they can never come to a consensus.
Some negotiations seem fair, but one side suffers a big loss.

小 斑 馬 的 領 悟

The Little Zebra's

Epiphany

農場主人在原野上看到一隻死去的母斑馬，旁邊趴著一隻剛生的小斑馬。

　　「可憐的小東西，大概難產，牠活了，媽媽卻死了。」農場主人把小斑馬帶回自家農場照顧。

　　農場裡有兩匹白馬，小斑馬總是跟在白馬身邊跑來跑去。

　　小斑馬也喜歡到水邊看自己的影子，一邊看一邊想：

　　「為什麼我身上有這些黑條紋，難看死了！我原本一定是隻白馬，莫名其妙地長了這些黑色的東西。」

　　小斑馬發現農場磨坊裡有一種白白的粉，牠總是撞開磨坊的門，到裡面打滾。

「看！我成了一隻白馬。」每次打完滾，小斑馬都得意地告訴自己：「我再也沒有髒兮兮的條紋了。」只是沒過多久，風吹掉了身上的麵粉，牠又成為一隻斑馬。

由於小斑馬總到磨坊闖禍，主人不得不把牠送給朋友。

朋友的農場裡有一匹大黑馬。

小斑馬起先躲著黑馬，但是漸漸覺得那黑馬，黑得真美、真純、真亮。牠又開始怨，自己身上為什麼有那麼多白色的條紋，牠想：「我原本應該是黑馬，只因為長了白條紋，所以變成這個醜樣子。」

小斑馬發現廚房後面有個煤堆，只要去那煤

堆裡打個滾，就能變成黑馬。

　　所以牠總是去打滾，弄得一身煤灰，把馬廄搞得髒兮兮。

　　新主人也受不了了，心想斑馬就是斑馬，怎麼馴養，也成不了家裡的馬。於是有一天，開著車，把小斑馬帶到曠野裡放生了。

　　「去！回到你原來的地方！」新主人把小斑馬趕下車，就揚長而去。

　　小斑馬嚇到了，站在一望無際的草原上，不知怎麼辦。突然，牠看到一片密密麻麻的影子在遠處移動。

　　小斑馬跟過去。天哪！居然是成千上萬隻像自己一樣的馬。

「你們是白馬還是黑馬？」小斑馬大聲問。

幾隻大斑馬抬起頭，不解地看看牠，其中一隻開口了：

「跟你一樣，我們不是白馬，也不是黑馬，是斑馬。」

小斑馬成年了，跟著那群斑馬徜徉於天地之間。

牠常得意地自言自語：

「斑馬就是斑馬，是最美麗的馬。我何必去羨慕別人呢？我真高興，自己沒有硬把自己裝扮成白馬或黑馬。」

A farm owner found a dead female zebra in the grasslands. Next to her was a newborn zebra.

"Poor thing. The birth must have been too difficult. The baby lived, but its mother died." The farm owner brought the little zebra back to his farm for care.

The farm had two white horses. The little zebra always galloped around with the white horses.

The little zebra also liked to go to the water and look at its own reflection. It would look and think: "Why does my body have these black stripes? They're so ugly! I must have been a white horse originally, and then somehow I grew these black marks."

The little zebra discovered that there was a kind of white

powder inside the farm's milling room. It often smashed the milling room's doors open to roll around in the white powder.

"Look! I've become a white horse," the little zebra would proudly tell itself every time after rolling in the powder. "I'll never have those dirty stripes again." But soon after, the wind would blow away the flour on its body, and it would become a little zebra again.

◉

Because the little zebra constantly made a mess in the milling room, the farm owner had no choice but to give the zebra to a friend.

The friend's farm had a large black horse.

The little zebra hid from the black horse at first, but it

increasingly thought the black horse's color was beautiful, pure, and shiny. It then began complaining to itself again, wondering why its own body had so many white stripes. It thought, "I was actually originally a black horse. Then I somehow grew these white stripes and became ugly."

The little zebra discovered that there was a pile of coal behind the kitchen. All it had to do was roll around in the coal, and it would become a black horse.

Therefore, it frequently went there to roll around. Its body would be covered in coal, which made the stables dirty every time.

⊙

The new owner could not stand the little zebra anymore either. He thought to himself, "A zebra will always be a zebra.

No degree of training can domesticate it to act like a horse."
Therefore, one day, the owner put the little zebra in his car,
and let it go into the wild.

"Go! Go back to where you came from!" The new owner
forced the little zebra out of the car and quickly departed.

The little zebra felt frightened. It stood in the grasslands,
which seemed endless, and it did not know what to do.
Suddenly, it saw a densely packed group of shadows moving
in the distance.

The little zebra ran over. Wow! There were tens of thousands
of horses that looked just like it.

"Are you white horses or black horses?" the little zebra loudly
asked.

A few adult zebras raised their heads and looked at it with confusion. One said, "We're the same as you. We're neither white nor black horses. We are zebras."

◉

The little zebra grew into adulthood, wandering between heaven and earth with the pack of zebras.

It often proudly muttered to itself: "Zebras are zebras, the most beautiful kind of horse. Why did I ever envy others? I'm so happy that I did not insist on pretending to be a white horse or a black horse."

藤 與 樹

●

The Vine and the Tree

藤子對樹說：

「你長那樣粗做什麼？難看死了！」

樹說：

「請你別纏著我，我好開始瘦身。」

The vine said to the tree, "Why did you grow to be this thick? It's awfully ugly!"

The tree said, "Please stop wrapping around me, so that I can become slimmer."

毛蟲的願望

The Caterpillar's Wish

　　有一隻毛蟲，覺得自己長得既醜陋，行動又不靈活，終日悶悶不樂，有一天憋不住了，去對上帝抱怨：

　　「上帝呀！您創造萬物固然神妙，但是我覺得您安排我的一生，卻不高明。您把我的一生分成兩個階段，不是既醜陋又遲鈍，就是既美麗又輕盈，使我在前一個階段被人嫌棄，後一個階段又被讚美。壞就壞到家，好又好得過火，這未免太不合理了。您何不平均一下，讓我現在雖然醜一點，卻能行動得輕巧些；以後當蝴蝶的時候，外

貌長得漂亮，但行動遲緩一點。這樣我作毛蟲和蝴蝶的兩個階段，不就都能過得很愉快了嗎？」

上帝笑笑說：「但是你有沒有想到，如果那樣做，你根本活不了多久。」

「為什麼呢？」毛蟲搖著大腦袋問。

「因為如果你有蝴蝶的美貌，卻只有毛蟲速度，一下子就被捉走了。」上帝說：「正因為你的行動遲緩，我才賜給你醜陋的外貌，使大家都不敢碰你，他們的不理不睬，對你只有好處沒有壞處啊。現在你還希望我採納你的構想嗎？」

「不！不！不！請維持您原來的安排吧！」毛蟲慌張地說：「現在我才知道，不論美麗與醜陋、輕盈與遲緩，只要由您創造，一定都是完美的！」

There was once a caterpillar who felt that its looks were too ugly and its movements were too slow. It was unhappy all the time. One day, it could no longer hold back its thoughts, and so it complained to God:

"God! The way You create living things is undoubtedly marvelous, but I feel that the way You arranged my life is not sensible. You split my life into two stages: one is ugly and slow, the other is beautiful and nimble. Everyone is disgusted with me in the first stage, and then everyone admires me in the second stage. I'm either extremely horrible or excessively wonderful; this does not make sense. Why don't You even things out, so that despite being ugly now, I can move nimbly. Later when I'm a butterfly, let me look beautiful, while moving more clumsily. Then wouldn't I be able to live happily in both my caterpillar and butterfly stages?"

God laughed and said, "But did you consider: if what you propose were true, you would not live for long."

"Why not?" the caterpillar asked, shaking its big head in confusion.

"If you had a butterfly's beauty but only a caterpillar's speed, then you would quickly be captured," God said. "It is because your movements are slow that I decided to grant you an ugly appearance, so that nobody dares to touch you. Their disregard for you is an advantage to you, not a disadvantage. Now, do you still wish for me to implement your idea?"

"No! No! No! Please stick with Your original plan!" the caterpillar said with panic. "Now I know—whether beautiful or ugly, nimble or slow—as long as I am created by You, I am perfect!"

誰 最 快 樂

Who Is Happier

貓對老鼠說：

「你的洞裡既窄又髒還潮溼，真是一貧如洗，可憐透了！」

老鼠對貓說：

「我的洞裡沒有貓，所以我很快樂。你的房子既寬又大，還有吃不完的東西，可是你抓不到老鼠，所以你不滿足。」

The cat said to the mouse, "Your hole is not only narrow, but also dirty and humid. You truly have nothing—pitiful to the extreme!"

The mouse said to the cat, "My hole also doesn't have cats, and therefore I'm very happy. Even though your house is wide and big and has more food than you could ever eat, you cannot catch a mouse. Therefore, you are unsatisfied."

小紙船與大海

The Paper Boat and the Sea

　　有個男孩摺了一隻小紙船，放在陰溝裡，吹了兩口氣。大概氣不夠強，小紙船動都沒動，男孩覺得無趣，就走了。

　　小紙船有了自由，開始打量四周，接著嘆口氣對陰溝說：

　　「你既窄又臭，噁心死了，實在跟我不配。你知道嗎？有一天我會變成真的帆船，在寬闊的海洋航行。」

　　陰溝笑笑說：

　　「別做夢了！你會爛在這裡，永遠變不成真的帆船。我卻會慢慢流，有一天成為大海。」

A boy made a small paper boat, put it in the gutter, and blew at it twice. Probably because he blew too weakly, the paper boat did not move at all. The boy got bored, so he left.

The paper boat had freedom now. It began sizing up its surroundings. Then it sighed and said to the gutter, "You are narrow and stinky. You're gross, and you're honestly unworthy of me. You know what? Someday, I will become a real sailboat and sail across the vast oceans."

The gutter laughed and said, "Stop dreaming! You will decay here, and you will never turn into a real sailboat. I, however, will slowly flow along and someday become a great sea."

魚 與 鉤 的 賭 局

●

A Bet Between

the Fish and the Hook

鉤和魚打賭。

鉤對魚說：

「你有本事的話，就把餌吃掉，把我吐出來。」

魚對鉤說：

「你有本事的話，就把餌保住，把我釣上去。」

結果 ——

魚咬下了餌，沒能吐出鉤。

鉤釣上了魚，沒能保住餌。

鉤說：「我們平手！」

The hook and the fish made a bet.

The hook said to the fish, "If you think you can beat me, then eat the bait but spit me out."

The fish said to the hook, "If you think you can beat me, then keep the bait but catch me."

The result was…

The fish bit the bait, but it could not spit out the hook.

The hook caught the fish, but it could not keep the bait.

The hook said, "It's a tie!"

井蛙望天
●
The Frog in the Well

　　有個孩子到井邊打水，當他正要把水桶往下垂的時候，突然從井底傳來一陣歌聲。

　　「是誰在裡面唱歌啊？」孩子趴在井邊大聲問。

「是我在唱歌！」一隻青蛙正腆著大肚皮，躺在水裡洗澡：「這井水真是太涼快、太乾淨、太甜美、太舒服了！使我高興得非哼上幾句不可！」

　　「哈！哈！哈！哈！」孩子幾乎笑彎了腰：「你真不愧是個井底之蛙，陷身在潮溼黑暗的井底，居然還很得意。讓我把你救出來吧！給你看看外面的世界，保證你只要瞧一眼，就再也不願回到井底。」

　　「謝謝您的好意，外面美麗的世界，您還是留著自己享用吧！我在井底已經很滿足了，不相信外面會更好。」

「怪不得大家都形容那些見識淺薄，沒看過世面的人為『井蛙望天』，你真是井蛙望天，才三尺不到的那麼一小塊天，就能讓你滿足了嗎？」

「我當然滿足，三尺不到的天也是天。你們的天是圓的，我的天也是圓的。再說，我這麼一隻小小的青蛙，何必要太大的天空，那樣太浪費了！」青蛙理直氣壯地說。

「可是你知道：晴朗時萬里青空，半晴時白雲舒捲，陰天時濃雲密布，黃昏時滿天彩霞的各種變幻嗎？」孩子說。

青蛙一笑：「但我也知道天上會降下豪雨，淹沒你的田園；颳起颱風，吹飛你的屋頂；打起閃電，嚇得你往被窩裡躲。」拍拍大肚皮：「可我都不怕，就算下傾盆大雨，不過是為我這可愛的池塘添半桶水！就算颳起十五級颱風，不過是給我吹吹風扇！就算滿天閃電，不過給我照照亮罷了！」指指上面，青蛙得意地說：「你別瞧不起我這塊天空喲！它雖然小，卻只有好處；你也別得意擁有大塊的天空喲！要想想它雖然給你好處，但也給你傷害。所以不要想擁有太多，得到太多反而帶來煩惱；更不要罵我井蛙望天，你又能看幾個天空呢？」

「好！好！好！算你會講話，我說不過你，現在請你讓開一點，我要打水了！」說完，孩子就將桶子拋了下去，在井底激起好大的水花。

　　「喂！客氣一點好不好！」青蛙大聲喊：「你說井底侷促得不成樣子，為什麼還來我這小地方打水？你說我生活得十分可憐，為什麼還來破壞我的寧靜？你說我是井蛙望天，擁有的天空不過三尺，可是當你說這句話的時候，正擋住了我的天空啊！」

A child went to a well to draw water. As he was about to lower the bucket, he suddenly heard a singing voice coming from the bottom of the well.

"Who is singing in there?" the child asked loudly, leaning over the edge of the well.

"I am the one singing!" said a frog, with his big white belly protruding, as he bathed in the water. "This well water is truly refreshing. It's so clean, wonderful, and comfortable! It makes me so happy; I can't help but sing!"

"Ha! Ha! Ha! Ha!" The child laughed so hard he almost fell over. "You really are a frog at the bottom of a well. You're trapped in a damp and dark place, but you're proud of it! Let me rescue you! I'll let you see this big wide world. I bet you'll take one look and faint from shock at the world's beauty, and you'll never want to go back to the bottom again!"

"Thank you for your kindness. You can save the beautiful outside world for yourself! I'm already very happy at the bottom of the well. I don't believe the outside can be better than this place."

"No wonder everyone describes people who are narrow-minded and inexperienced as 'frogs in a well, looking at the sky.' You truly are a frog in a well, looking at the sky. Your little sky is less than three feet in diameter, but it's enough to satisfy you?"

"Of course I am satisfied. A three-foot sky is still a sky. Your sky is round, and my sky is round too! Moreover, I am a tiny frog. Why would I need a gigantic sky? That would be a waste!" said the frog righteously.

"But do you know: on a clear day, how it looks clear for miles? When it's partly sunny, how the white clouds billow? When it's cloudy, how the dense clouds cover everything? When it's dusk, how the multi-colored sky changes like magic?" said the child.

The frog smiled and said, "I also know that when a storm rains down from the sky, it floods your fields. Hurricanes blow your roofs off, and lightning scares you running into your blankets." He patted his big belly and continued, "But I'm not afraid of any of that. Even when there's pouring rain, it just adds half a bucket of water to this adorable pond of mine! Even if there were a Category 15 typhoon, it would merely feel like a fan on my face! Even when the sky is full of lightning, it only helps to brighten my space!" Pointing upward, the frog proudly said, "Don't belittle my piece of sky! Although it is small, it is full of benefits. Don't be too proud of having your big sky either! Think about how despite its benefits, it also hurts you. Therefore, don't be greedy; having too much might bring trouble. Also, don't use 'a frog in a well, looking at the sky' as an insult. How many skies can you see at one time?"

"Ok! Ok! Ok! You're better at talking; I can't argue with you. Now please move over because I'm about to draw water!" The child immediately threw down his bucket, making a huge splash at the bottom of the well.

"Hey! Can you be more polite please!" the frog shouted. "If you say the bottom of my well is horribly cramped, then why do you draw water from this small place? If you say my life is extremely unfortunate, then why do you come disturb my bit of peace? You say I'm a frog in a well, looking at the sky, having only a three-foot sky. But as you're saying this, you're actually blocking my sky!"

天 空 是 誰 的

Who Owns the Sky

56

黎明和黃昏總是為了誰比較漂亮吵架，最後
決定請太陽來開會，大家劃分勢力範圍。

57

黎明先發言：「我們把天空劃成三份吧！誰也不多，誰也不少。每天早上，我在東邊的天空展現黃色的朝暉，我最美，所以東邊的天空屬於我。」

　　黃昏接著說：「每天晚上我在西邊的天空鋪陳紅色的晚霞，我最美，所以西邊的天空歸我。」

　　然後他們一起轉頭看太陽說：「中間最好的位置留給您，請您在中間做個緩衝，免得我們兩個打架。」

　　太陽笑笑說：「謝謝你們的好意，可是我不想參加耶！你們還是請黑夜來幫忙吧！黑夜不是也在你們中間嗎？」

　　「黑夜在哪裡？要怎麼請？」黎明和黃昏問。

　　太陽說：「不必請。我一走，它就來了。」

The dawn and the dusk always fought over who was prettier. In the end, they decided to hold a meeting with the sun, to define everyone's scope of authority.

The dawn spoke first: "Let's divide the sky into three parts! No one would have more, and no one would have less. Every morning, I display a yellow glow in the eastern sky, and I am the most beautiful. Therefore, the eastern part of the sky is mine."

The dusk spoke next: "Every evening, I decorate the western sky with a red sunset, and I am the most beautiful. Therefore, the western part of the sky is mine."

Then, they both turned to look at the sun and said, "We're saving the best spot in the middle for you. Please be a buffer in the middle, to prevent us two from fighting."

The sun smiled and said, "Thank you for your kindness, but I don't feel like participating! You can ask the night to come help! Isn't the night between you two as well?"

"Where is the night? How do we invite it?" the dawn and the dusk asked.

The sun said, "No need to invite. As soon as I leave, it will come."

等你回頭

For You to Turn Back

蝴蝶對花朵說：「我為你傳布花粉，是因為以前做毛蟲的時候，咬壞你太多的葉子，我對你有太多的虧欠。」

花朵對蝴蝶笑笑：「別這麼說！我也要謝謝你當時沒把我的葉子吃光，讓我還有能力開花。而且我早知道你會改變，現在打扮得這麼美麗，就是為了等你回頭。」

The butterfly said to the flower, "I help you spread pollen because, back when I was a caterpillar, I bit and damaged too many of your leaves. I owe you too much."

The flower smiled and said to the butterfly, "Don't say such things! I also want to thank you for not eating all my leaves back then, so that I was still able to bloom. Besides, I always knew you would change. I have dressed up this beautifully, only to wait for you to turn back."

十二個孩子

Twelve Children

　　某地突然流行一種怪病，患者都是幼兒，由於過去沒有那樣的病歷，症狀又惡化得極快，使得群醫束手，幼兒一個接一個地死去。

　　有位富翁的獨子也染上這種病，富翁四處打聽，終於發現那病是從國外傳來的，只有一種藥可以救，而且一劑見效。只是那種藥非常昂貴，效期又短，即使用乾冰保存，也只能維持七十二小時，加上是特別製作，一次必須購買整打包裝。

　　「我只需要一劑！」富翁打電報問。

　　「一劑不賣，必須一次訂十二劑！」回電毫不通融。

為了救愛兒的命，雖然對富翁而言，這十二劑也是極大的負擔，他還是訂了。

　　特效藥立刻空運過來，但是就在到達的前一刻，富翁的獨子卻已經等不及而斷氣。富翁的妻子撫屍痛哭，卻見丈夫衝出門去，置愛兒的屍體於不顧。

　　原來富翁衝去機場拿藥，再晝夜不停地驅車到各地醫院詢問，遇見與他愛兒患同樣病的孩子，便留下一劑藥離開，兩天兩夜不食不眠，他終於把藥在過時之前送給了十二個垂危的病童，但是當他蒼白著臉跨進家門時，卻被不知情的妻子狠狠打了一記耳光：「你這無情的東西，怪不得絕子！」

富翁並沒有絕子，他有
了十二個孩子，經常繞在膝
下，全鄉的人都說：那十二
個孩子的命是他賜予的。

There was an epidemic of a strange disease that only affected young children. It was a novel disease, and the symptoms worsened extremely quickly. Doctors were helpless, and children were dying one after the other.

A wealthy man's only son also contracted this disease. The wealthy man searched for answers everywhere and discovered that this disease originated from another country. One cure existed; one dose of an antiserum was all that he needed. However, the antiserum was very expensive and would lose its effectiveness in 72 hours, even if kept on ice. The antiserum was also difficult to cultivate, and so it had to be purchased by the batch.

"I only need one dose!" the wealthy man wrote in his message.

"We don't sell single doses. The minimum order is 12 in a batch," the other side replied rigidly.

Even for such a wealthy man, purchasing 12 doses would be a financial burden. But for the sake of saving his son's life, he placed the order.

The antiserum was immediately shipped by air. On the day it was set to arrive, the wealthy man's son passed away. The wealthy man's wife sobbed over the son's body, but she saw her husband rush out the door, with no regard for their deceased son.

It turns out that the wealthy man was rushing to the airport to pick up the antiserum. Then, day and night, he drove to various hospitals and asked to meet children with the same disease that his son had. He gave each of them one dose of the antiserum. For two days and two nights, he neither slept nor ate. Before the antiserum expired, he was able to distribute the 12 doses to 12 dying children. But when he finally arrived home, tired and pale, he was unexpectedly greeted by a hard slap in the face from his wife: "You're so heartless—no wonder you have no more children!"

However, the wealthy man did have children. He had 12. They often surrounded him at his knees, and the whole village said, "He gave those 12 children their lives."

姑 息 養 奸

●

To Tolerate Evil

────────────

　　小李到裱畫店當學徒已經一年多了，技術學到不少，生活起居也滿意，唯一困擾的是師傅姑息養奸的態度。

　　那被養的「奸」是老鼠，小李活到二十歲，還從來沒見過那麼肥大又猖狂的老鼠。他在桌上裱畫，老鼠就在桌下追逐，且發出吱吱的叫聲；尤其令他痛恨的，是每天晚上剛躺下，就聽見老鼠跳上裱畫桌，喝盆裡的漿糊，還得意地打飽嗝。

　　每當小李說要清除鼠患，師傅都笑說：「反正牠又不咬畫，漿糊多的是，讓牠們吃一點也沒關係，這些老鼠挺識趣，你幾時見牠們在漿糊裡拉過半粒屎？」

　　聽這番話，小李就更有氣了，因為漿糊是他調的，變成他在伺候老鼠。有一回被老鼠吃消夜的聲音吵得睡不著覺，拿著掃把下去追，居然還被師傅訓斥一頓，說如果碰傷了畫，豈非連老鼠都不如。

　　報復的機會終於來了，師傅在鄉下的家裡有事，帶著老小離開一個星期。

　　當天晚上，小李就把剩下的漿糊全倒了，並把盆子裡外刷洗得一乾二淨。

　　「把你們餓扁，看你們滾不滾！」小李得意地想。

　　夜裡，他很清楚地聽見老鼠們跳上跳下和吱

吱討論的聲音，又夢到人鼠大戰的場面，當然最
後是小李獲勝。

　　師傅終於回來了，一進門，小李就報告自己
清鼠的成績，沒想到師傅頓時蹙了眉，先是低下
頭沉吟，跟著叫小李把立在牆邊的裱畫板全翻過
來。

　　才翻開第一塊，小李就嚇呆了，豆大的汗珠
從額頭滲出，滴在那被咬嚙得面目全非的畫上。

Li had been an apprentice at the framing store for over a year. He had learned quite a bit of technique, and he was satisfied with the living conditions. His one complaint was Master's tendency to tolerate evil and therefore abet it.

That "evil" was rats. In his 20 years of life, Li had never seen such fat and ferocious rats. While he framed paintings on top of the table, rats chased each other under the table while squeaking. What he hated the most was how every night, as soon as he went to bed, he heard the rats jump on top of the table and drink the bowl of framing paste; they even burped proudly.

Every time Li said he wanted to exterminate the rats, Master always smiled and said, "They don't bite the paintings anyway. And we have plenty of paste, so it's ok if they eat some. These rats are quite prudent. When have you ever seen them leave even half a dropping in the paste?"

Upon hearing that, Li felt angrier. Since he was the one who mixed the paste, this meant that he was serving the rats. One time, the rats were so noisily eating their midnight snack that he couldn't fall asleep, and he chased them with a broom. But Master actually scolded him and said that if he had damaged the paintings, then he would be worse than a rat.

The opportunity for revenge finally came. Master needed to go back to the countryside, and so he left for the week with his entire family.

That night, Li threw out the remainder of the paste, and he brushed the bowl until it was perfectly clean on all sides.

"That should starve you. Let's see if you leave!" Li thought to himself proudly.

In the middle of the night, he clearly heard the rats jumping up and down and having squeaky discussions. He also dreamed of a great battle between humans and rats, and of course Li was the victor.

Master finally returned. As soon as Master walked through the door, Li reported his success in getting rid of the rats. To Li's surprise, Master suddenly frowned. First, he lowered his head and groaned. Then, he told Li to flip over all the framing boards that were leaning against the wall.

Upon flipping just the first board, Li froze in shock. Sweat beads as big as beans dripped down from his forehead, dripping onto the painting which had been bitten beyond recognition.

富翁之死

●

Death of a Rich Man

　　有個富翁在急流中翻了船，爬到石頭上大喊救命。

　　一個年輕人奮不顧身地划船去救，但是山洪下瀉的湍流，使他的船進行非常緩慢。

　　「快呀！」富翁高喊：「如果你救了我，我送你一千塊！」

　　船仍然移動緩慢。

　　「用力划啊！如果你划到，我給你兩千塊！」

　　青年奮力地划著，但是既要向前，又要抗拒水流的阻力，船速仍然難以加快！

　　「水在漲，你用力呀！」富翁嘶聲喊著：「我給你五千塊！」洪流已經快淹到他站立的地方。

青年的船緩緩靠近，但仍然嫌慢。

「我給你一萬塊，拚命呀！」富翁的腳已經泡在水裡。

但是船速反而更慢了。

「我給你五萬……」富翁的話還沒有說完，已經被一個大浪打下岩石，轉眼捲入洪流，失去了蹤影。

青年頹喪地回到岸上，蒙頭痛哭：

「我當初只想救他一命，他卻說要送我錢，而且一次又一次地增加。我心想，只要划慢一點點，就可能多幾萬塊的收入。哪裡知道就因為慢了這麼一下，讓他被水沖走，是我害死了他啊！」青年捶著頭：「但是當我心裡只有義，而沒有利的時候，他為什麼要說給我錢呢？」

A rich man's boat capsized in rapids. Clambering up some rocks in the middle of the river, he yelled for help.

Undaunted by the dangerous conditions, a young man rushed out on his rowboat to the rescue, but the torrential turbulence made it difficult to advance.

"Hurry up!" the rich man yelled. "I'm rich! If you save me, I will give you a thousand dollars!"

The boat moved slowly, nonetheless.

"Row harder! If you row to me, I will give you two thousand dollars!"

The young man rowed with all his might, but it was hard to move forward while fighting against the current. The boat could not go faster!

"The water is rising, come on!" the rich man yelled hysterically. "I'll give you five thousand dollars!" The rapids were becoming more violent, almost reaching where he stood.

The young man's boat was gradually getting closer, yet still moving too slowly.

"I'll give you ten thousand dollars! Row harder!" The rich man's feet were already under water.

However, the boat moved even slower.

"I'll give you fifty thousand…" Before the rich man could finish his sentence, he was knocked off the rocks and disappeared under the swirling rapids.

Hopeless, the young man rowed back to the riverbank and broke down sobbing:

"I just wanted to save his life at first, but he kept offering money—more and more money! I thought if I rowed a bit slower, then maybe I could earn tens of thousands more. How could I have known that by slowing down that one bit, I let the water take him away! I was the one who killed him!" The young man pounded himself on the head. "But when I was just doing what my heart knew was right—when benefiting myself never crossed my mind—why did he have to offer me money?"

對付採花賊

Dealing with
Nectar Thieves

小陶和老馮雖然是農場的鄰居，但很少講話。因為小陶有一天在她的果園裡被蜜蜂螫了，猜想蜜蜂一定是從老馮的養蜂場飛過來，跑去要老馮賠醫藥費。老馮非但不賠，還笑小陶搽太多香水招蜂引蝶。從此兩人結下樑子，誰也不理誰。

　　這天小陶上超市，看見架子上不同品牌的蜂蜜，有一種特貴，細看，竟然是老馮的出品，就問為什麼這牌子貴得多？

　　「您連這個都不知道啊？」店員瞪大了眼睛說：「好吃啊！這牌子蜂蜜特別香，有水蜜桃的味道」。還找了瓶樣品，讓小陶嚐嚐。果然！有水蜜桃的香味。

小陶回家愈想愈氣：「老馮的蜂場在隔壁，我種的又是一大片桃園，每年春天桃花盛開，免費讓老馮的蜜蜂來採花，好像女兒被非禮，便宜全讓老馮占了。」

　　接著小陶就去找老馮理論，要分老馮收入的三成。

　　老馮又冷笑：「你不高興，用網子把桃樹罩起來啊！我的蜜蜂有幾百萬，愛飛哪裡飛哪裡，我可管不了。」

　　小陶氣得幾夜睡不好覺，終於想出個妙計，她上網放消息：我每年春天噴殺蟲藥，雖然農藥一下子就揮發了，不會影響結果，但是來採蜜的可得小心，就算蜜蜂不死，採去的蜜也帶農藥。
吃不得！

　　果然，消息才出去，老馮的蜂蜜就一落千丈，
連一瓶也賣不掉。

　　老馮不得不認輸，匆匆忙忙把養蜂場搬走。

　　問題是，隔年小陶也出了問題，明明桃花依
然盛放，只因為不像往年有大批蜜蜂授粉，結成
的桃子少得多。而且大家再也不買她的桃子，說
小陶農藥噴得狠，把老馮都嚇跑了，桃子還能吃
嗎？

Although Ms. Tao and Mr. Feng owned neighboring farms, they rarely spoke to one another. This is because Ms. Tao was once stung by a bee while working in her orchard. She guessed that the bee must have flown over from Mr. Feng's bee farm, so she ran over to demand that he pay for medicine. Mr. Feng not only refused to pay, but he even joked that Ms. Tao put on too much perfume and therefore attracted bees. From then on, the two neighbors officially became foes and no longer acknowledged each other.

On this day, Ms. Tao was at a supermarket and saw that among all the various brands of honey on the shelf, one brand was particularly expensive. Upon taking a closer look, she realized that it was produced by Mr. Feng. She wondered aloud why this brand was so much pricier than the others.

"You don't know about this?" The sales associate stared in disbelief. "It's delicious! This brand of honey is especially fragrant, with the essence of peaches." She found a sample for Ms. Tao to try. Sure enough! It was fragrant like peaches.

Back at home, the more Ms. Tao thought about it, the angrier she felt: "Mr. Feng's bee farm is next door, and I have a big peach orchard. Every spring when the peach blossoms bloom, Mr. Feng's bees come over and forage for free. It's like letting my daughters be defiled, while Mr. Feng takes advantage of it all."

Ms. Tao then went over to reason with Mr. Feng. She wanted one-third of Mr. Feng's profits.

Mr. Feng sneered: "If you're upset, then put a net over your peach trees! I have millions of bees. They fly wherever they want. I can't control them."

For many nights, Ms. Tao was too angry to sleep well. She finally thought of a trick. She announced online: "I spray pesticides every spring. Although the pesticides evaporate quickly and do not affect the fruits, all foragers should beware. Even if the bees don't die, the nectar that they collect contains pesticides. Not safe to eat!"

As expected, as soon as the announcement was posted, Mr. Feng's honey sales plummeted. He could not sell a single jar.

Mr. Feng had no choice but to surrender. He hurriedly moved his bee farm elsewhere.

However, the following year, Ms. Tao also had a problem on her hands. The peach blossoms bloomed wonderfully per usual, but because there weren't the same multitudes of bees serving as pollinators, the trees produced far fewer peaches than in previous years. Besides, people no longer bought her peaches. They said Ms. Tao sprays pesticides so heavily that she scared Mr. Feng away. How could the peaches be safe to eat?

三把麵條

Three Bundles of Noodles

　　這是發生在九〇年代的故事：一個由美國華人組織的慈善團體，派員到中國的偏遠地區考察。

　　十幾位平日養尊處優的中年女士，在愛心的鼓舞下，居然跋山涉水到與世隔絕的山村。當他們知道那裡的孩子每天都得走幾個小時的山路去上學，立刻提議：「我們出錢為你們蓋個學校吧！」

　　村人興奮極了！有人志願敲石頭奠基，有人要去挖泥土燒磚，有揹著孩子的婦人說要幫忙墾地，還有一位獨居的老太太說她想捐錢，可是沒錢，想出力又沒力氣，只能捐點吃的給遠道來的好心人，於是拿出了她僅有的三把乾麵條。

「問題是，鋼筋水泥怎麼運進來？」正興高采烈的時候，有人提出：「咱們村子對外只有一條羊腸小道，平常走路都難，車子根本進不來啊！」

大家都怔住了，慈善團體的人也沒辦法，只好失望地離開，轉往附近另一個村子。

「我們也沒路啊！」另一個村子的人也直嘆氣：「我們是被城市遺忘的可憐的小村子。」

慈善團體的人又失望地走了，但是他們不死心，既然千辛萬苦地來到深山，非要找個貧窮村落，為孩子蓋學校不可。

他們找到第三個山村。

「我們比那兩個村子還窮、還偏僻，他們被遺

忘，我們更被遺忘了。」村長召集村民開了半天
會，也一籌莫展。

　　正搖頭嘆氣的時候，突然有個年輕人舉手：
「人家遺忘我們，我們不能遺忘自己。」

　　·年之後，鋼筋水泥居然順利地運進三個村
子。

　　是一包包揹、一綑綑抬嗎？

　　不！是用貨車載進去的。因為三個村子的村
民齊心協力，開了一條通往外面的道路。

　　三個鄉村小學同時落成了！三個山村的經濟
也大大改善了，以前運不出去，只能爛在路邊的
蔬果，一車車賣到城市，外面的物資也源源不絕
地運進村子。

　　好多早先為孩子搬出去的人都回來了：「自己
家邊就有學校，我們當然回家。」

　　以前山裡請不到老師，現在也不成問題了。
因為好多大學剛畢業的年輕人，志願去教書：「那
裡真美，真是被遺忘的世外桃源！」

　　其中一所學校的校名很特殊，用的是那捐麵
條老太太的名字。

This is a story that took place in the 1990s. A nonprofit organization founded by Chinese-Americans sent its members on an expedition to a remote region of China.

More than 10 middle-aged women, who normally enjoyed wealthy and comfortable lifestyles, were inspired by the love in their hearts to trek through mountains and waters to a mountain village that was isolated from the world. When they realized that the children there had to hike for hours each day to attend school, they immediately proposed, "We'll donate the money for you to build a school!"

The villagers were extremely excited! There were people who volunteered to hammer stones and lay the foundation. There were people who wanted to dig up dirt and make bricks. There were women, carrying children on their backs, who said they wanted to help reclaim land. There was also a lonely old lady who said she wanted to give money but had no money and wanted to help with labor but had no energy. She could only contribute some food for the kind visitors, so she offered all that she had: three bundles of dry noodles.

"The problem is… how do we transport the cement in?" someone said, just as everyone was elated. "Our village only has one small windy path to the outside. It's difficult to even walk on. There's no way for cars to come in!"

Everyone was flabbergasted. The nonprofit members had no solution either, so they disappointedly departed and walked toward another village nearby.

◉

"We don't have a road either!" The people of the other village sighed repeatedly. "We are a pitiful little village that has been forgotten by the city."

The nonprofit members disappointedly departed again. However, they were unwilling to give up. Since they had gone through all this trouble to come this far into the mountains, they needed to find an impoverished village where they could build a school for children.

They came upon a third village.

"We're even poorer and even more out of the way than those other two villages. If they have been forgotten, then we have been even more forgotten." The village chief gathered the villagers for a long meeting, but to no avail.

Just as everyone was shaking their heads and sighing, a young villager suddenly raised his hand and said, "Other people may have forgotten us, but we cannot forget ourselves."

⊙

One year later, the cement was successfully transported into the three villages.

Was it carried in bag by bag, bundle by bundle?

No! It came in on trucks. The people of the three villages had worked together and constructed a road to the outside world.

The schools in all three villages were completed at the same time! The economies of the three mountain villages also greatly improved. In the past, excess fruits and vegetables could not be transported outward, so they rotted along the wayside. Now, they were sold in truckloads to the city, and supplies from the city were constantly brought to the villages.

Many people, who had moved away for their children's sake, now came back: "There's a school right next door now. Of course we're coming home."

The mountain villages had trouble hiring teachers in the past, but that was no longer an issue because many recent college graduates volunteered to teach there: "That place is beautiful. It is truly a utopia that had been forgotten!"

One of the schools had a very special name. It was named after the old lady who had donated noodles.

富翁的大房簷

The Rich Man's Eaves

　　從前有位善心的富翁，蓋了一棟大房子，他
特別要求營造的師傅，把四周的房簷建得特別
長，使貧苦無家的人，能在下面暫時躲避風雪。
　　房子建成了，果然有許多窮人聚集簷下，他
們擺攤子做買賣，甚至生火煮飯賣小吃，嘈雜的
人聲與油煙使富翁不堪其擾，不悅的家人也常與
寄在簷下者爭吵。

　　冬天，有個老人在簷下凍死了，大家交口罵
富翁不仁。
　　夏天，一場颱風，別人的房子都沒事，富翁

的房子因爲屋簷特長，居然被掀了頂。村人們都
說這是惡有惡報。

　　重修屋頂時，富翁要求只建小小的房簷，因
爲他明白：施人餘蔭總讓受施者有仰人鼻息的自
卑感，結果由自卑變成了敵對。

　　富翁把錢捐給慈善機構，並蓋了一間小房子，
所能庇蔭的範圍遠比以前的房簷小，但是四面有
牆，是棟正式的屋子。許多無家可歸的人，都在
其中獲得暫時的庇護，並在臨走時，問這棟房子
是哪位善人捐建。

　　沒有幾年，富翁成為最受歡迎的人，即使在
他死後，人們還繼續受他的恩澤並紀念他。

There was once a man who was rich and kind, and he built himself a mansion. He asked his construction team to make the overhanging eaves on all four sides especially wide, so that poor and homeless people could temporarily stay underneath and be sheltered from snowstorms.

The mansion was completed, and many poor people indeed gathered under its eaves. They set up stalls to buy and sell goods. They even cooked there and sold food. The noisy crowds and greasy fumes were too annoying for the rich man to bear, and his unhappy family members often got into arguments with the people under their eaves.

That winter, an old man froze to death under the eaves. Everyone gossiped and said the rich man was heartless.

That summer, there was a typhoon. Other people's houses were unaffected, but because the rich man's eaves were especially wide, his roof blew off. The townspeople said bad things come to the wicked.

When reconstructing his roof, the rich man requested small overhanging eaves because he now understood. When he gives people his leftovers, the recipients feel that they're living at his mercy and feel inferior to him. Feeling inferior turns into feeling bitter toward him.

The rich man donated money to a charity and built a small house. Its sheltered area was much smaller than the previous mansion's eaves, but it had four walls and was a proper house. Many homeless people found temporary refuge in that house, and upon leaving, they would ask who was so kind as to donate money and build it.

Just a few years later, the rich man became the most beloved man in the town. After he passed away, people continued to benefit from what he built, and they commemorated him.

獵鷹與野兔

The Falcon and the Hare

獵鷹抓到一隻野兔。

「大王！求求您饒了我的命吧！」兔子哀求：

「野地裡有許多田鼠，皮薄而肉嫩，一次一隻，

正合您用。如果您饒我不死，我一定幫您去掏田
鼠的洞穴，把他們趕出來，供您獵取。」

「你的主意實在不錯，問題是要抓你的不是
我，而是獵人，我只是聽命辦事而已，獵人不要
田鼠，所以我不能放你。」獵鷹回答。

「那您就更不應該抓我了，大王！」野兔掙扎
著扭過頭：「您知道嗎？那獵人是殺您父母的仇
家，他射死了您的雙親、搗毀了您的家，把您偷
回去養大，再驅使您為他做工，您應該報仇才對
呀！何況您已經把我父母抓去給獵人烤吃了，又
何忍再犧牲我呢？」

「你講得真有道理，可是我問你，如果今天
我的遭遇換成你，你能做一隻獵兔嗎？所以我抓

你，只因為我是獵鷹；你被殺，只能怪你是隻兔子。」獵鷹笑著說：「至於恩仇，什麼是恩仇呢？田鼠既是你的表親，又是你的鄰居，你們天天見面，不是相處得很好嗎？而今只為了保自己一命，你居然要去毀他們的家，驅他們來送死。獵人殺了我的父母，我不也殺了你的父母嗎？獵人把我養大，至今供我吃住，而我卻從未對你好過；我把你抓去交差，只是犧牲個不識相的兔子，而你叫田鼠送死，卻是出賣親友，到底誰才是不義的呢？」說完便啄出兔子的眼睛吞下去，並把兔子獻給了獵人。

A falcon caught a hare.

"King! Please spare my life!" the hare begged. "The fields are full of field mice. They have thin skin and tender meat. One per serving would be perfect for you. If you let me live, I promise I'll go disturb their holes, so that they come out for you to catch."

"That's a great idea indeed. The problem is I'm not the one who wants to catch you. I'm just obeying the hunter's commands. The hunter doesn't want field mice. Therefore, I can't let you go," the falcon replied.

"That's all the more reason to not capture me, king!" the

hare said, as it struggled to turn its head around. "Don't you know? That hunter is your enemy. He killed your parents, destroyed your home, kidnapped you to raise you, and now he commands you to work for him. You should take revenge! Furthermore, you already captured my parents for the hunter to roast and eat. How can you have the heart to sacrifice me too?"

"Your argument makes sense, but let me ask you something. If my misfortunes had befallen you instead, could you have become a rabbit who hunts? Therefore, I catch you because I am a falcon; you get killed only because you are a hare." The falcon smiled and continued: "As for revenge, what is gratitude and what is revenge? Field mice are your relatives and also your neighbors. You see each other every day. Don't you get along well? But today, just to save yourself, you are willing to destroy their homes and drive them out to die. The hunter killed my parents indeed, but didn't I kill your parents? The hunter raised me, and he gives me food and shelter. I, on the other hand, have never been nice to you. If I capture you to fulfill my duty, then I would be sacrificing an ignorant hare. But if you trick the field mice into getting killed, then you would be betraying your friends and relatives. So, who is the immoral one?"

Upon finishing its speech, the falcon pecked out the hare's eyes and swallowed them. Then, it gave the hare to the hunter.

牛與鷺鷥

●

The Cow and the Heron

牛對鷺鷥說：

「妳站在我的背上，看得比我還遠，我真不服氣。」

鷺鷥對牛說：

「跟我飛的時候相比，你的背是最矮的地方，我還真有點委屈。」

The cow said to the heron, "You stand on my back, so you can see farther than I can. I feel really bitter."

The heron said to the cow, "Compared to when I'm flying, your back is the lowest of all places. I actually feel a bit wronged."

偉大的老虎

The Mighty Tiger

老虎和猴子聊天。

「聽說人類是由你們猴子變的，但我勸你千萬不要變成人。」老虎指著猴子說。

「為什麼？」猴子詫異地問：「人不是萬物之靈嗎？他們的食、衣、住、行，樣樣都比我們強。」

「真是笑話！」老虎大吼了一聲，嚇得猴子差點從樹上摔下來。「你應該說人類的食、衣、住、行，沒有一樣及得上我。你可知道人類吃東西有多麻煩？

單單以麵包來說吧,從麥子的播種、施肥、除蟲、
收割、碾粉到發酵、燒烤,就不知要經過多少人
的手。可是我呢?我不必靠同類的幫助,自己就
能找到東西吃,而且還常吃不完呢!」

「您怎不想想人類吃東西麻煩，是因為他們講究呢？」猴子問。

「算了吧！他們不是講究，而是因為體質太差。吃生的怕拉肚子，只吃肉又恐油膩；吃少了怕營養不良，吃多了又怕發福。」老虎拍了拍胸膛：「你看看我們老虎，有沒有因為肉吃太多，而肥得要進醫院的？有沒有因為不吃水果蔬菜，而缺乏維他命 C 的？人類跟我們老虎比起來，真是差太多了！」

「對！對！對！人類的『食』，真是遠不如您。」猴子服氣地說：「您再談談衣吧！似乎所有的動物，只有人類會做衣服穿。」

「那也是因為他們差啊！」老虎笑著說：「人

類穿衣服，是因為他們天生光溜溜的，沒有衣服一定會凍死，所以不得不穿。如果他們能天生有我這身皮毛，還用得著花那許多功夫紡紗、織布、量身、剪裁嗎？」

「可是人類穿衣服還有一個目的，是為了裝飾、美觀、舒適啊！」猴子打斷老虎的話：「聽說他們的衣服很值錢呢！」

「胡說！」老虎突然火冒三丈：「他們的衣服再漂亮，又能美得過我的天然衣服嗎？他們的衣服再舒適，又能比我的皮毛更合身嗎？他們的衣服再值錢，又能貴過我的這件嗎？要是他們自己真能做出最好的料子，也用不著千方百計來搶我這件虎皮大衣了！」

「真是太有道理了！」猴子猛鼓掌，但是鼓了一陣，突然想到：「您的食和衣雖然比人類強，可是他們住的卻比您好啊！」

　　「別開玩笑了！」老虎突然又大笑起來：「人們羨慕我還來不及呢！聽說他們在城裡仿照我住的樣式，蓋了許多『人造山洞』，偏偏他們的技術又不行，結果弄得糟透了，使得許多人到假日，寧可跑到野外露營，也不願留在家裡。」

　　「人類的房子為什麼不好呢？」

　　「他們的水泥洞，一個連著一個，一間疊著一間，東家吵、西家鬧，戶戶不安寧。同時他們的水泥洞不像我的老虎洞能夠自由出入，而是幾十家共用一個大門，如果我是獵人去抓他們哪，只怕他們半個都跑不掉。再舉個簡單的例子吧！只聽說人類大樓失火，一死就是幾十人，總沒見過森林大火時，有老虎在洞裡被燒死吧？」老虎笑得直喘氣。

「真是太有道理了！還是老虎的科學進步。可是談到『行』呢？沒聽說老虎開汽車啊！」猴子說。

「人類也是因為自己身體差，既跑不快，又行不遠，才不得不開車的。你要知道，他們開的車子，並不是開車的人自己造的，一輛車子聽說要經過好幾百人的手呢！而且機器故障不能開，油用完了不能開，沒有駕駛執照不能開，路況不好也不能開，就算都成了，還會出車禍。」老虎得意地說：「你總沒聽說老虎撞老虎，一撞就死幾十隻吧？」

　　「對！對！對！對！對……」猴子一連說了十幾個對，點了幾十個頭，但是就在這時候，遠處突然傳來一聲槍響。

　　「糟了！人來了！我得跑了！」老虎連「再見」都來不及說，就一溜煙地衝向森林的深處。

　　「喂！」猴子大聲喊：「您不是說人類什麼都不如老虎嗎？可是您為什麼怕他們呢？」

　　「因為他們懂得守望相助、分工合作啊！」老虎的聲音隱約地從遠處傳來。

A tiger and a monkey were chatting.

"I heard that humans evolved from you monkeys, but I advise you to please not turn into a human," the tiger said, pointing at the monkey.

"Why not?" asked the monkey with astonishment. "Aren't humans the masters of everything? Their food, clothing, housing, and transportation are all superior to ours."

"What a joke!" The tiger roared so loudly that the monkey almost fell out of the tree. "You should say that humans' food, clothing, housing, and transportation are nowhere near my level. Do you know how much trouble humans go through just to eat something? Let's take bread for example. From planting seeds to fertilizing to spraying pesticides to harvesting, then making grain into flour and fermenting and baking, who knows how many people must be involved! As for me? I don't need help from any fellow tigers to get food, and I often even have leftovers!"

"Have you considered that humans go through all that trouble for food because they have sophisticated taste?" the monkey asked.

"Oh please! They're not sophisticated; they're weak. If they only ate raw food, then they would have diarrhea. If they only ate meat, then they would have heart disease. When they eat too little, they're afraid of malnutrition. When they eat too much, they're afraid of getting fat!" The tiger patted himself on the chest and continued: "Look at us tigers. Are any of us obese or hospitalized for eating too much meat? Are any of us lacking Vitamin C from not eating fruits and vegetables? Compared to tigers, humans are not even close!"

◉

"Yes, you are right! Humans are far inferior to you when it comes to food," the monkey said, fully convinced. "Let's talk about clothing though! It seems like humans are the only animals that can make clothes."

"That is also because they are weak!" the tiger said with a laugh. "Humans wear clothes because they were born naked. Without clothes, they would freeze to death, so they don't have a choice. If they were born with a coat like mine, then would they still go through all that effort of spinning, sewing, measuring, and tailoring?"

"But humans have other reasons for wearing clothes. They want fashion, beauty, comfort!" The monkey interrupted the tiger. "I heard that their clothes can be very expensive!"

"Nonsense!" shouted the tiger, suddenly very angry. "Their clothes may be beautiful, but are they more beautiful than my natural clothing? Can their clothes be more comfortable than my form-fitting coat? Can their clothes be more expensive than what I am wearing? If humans could really make the best fabrics on their own, then they wouldn't bother with all the tricks and traps to steal my tiger coat!"

⊙

"That totally makes sense!" The monkey applauded vigorously, but then it wondered: "Your food and clothing are superior, but humans have better housing than you do!"

"You're kidding!" The tiger was suddenly laughing again.

"Humans are the ones envying me! I heard that in their cities, they try to imitate my way of living by building 'man-made caves.' Their technique must be awful, and they've made such a mess that many humans would rather go camping in the wild on holidays, rather than stay at home."

"What's wrong with humans' homes?"

"Their concrete caves are all connected, one on top of the other. You can hear shouting from your eastern neighbor and partying from your western neighbor; nobody feels at peace. Also, their concrete caves don't allow for freedom of movement like my tiger cave does. A hundred families share one door! If I were a hunter going there to catch them, nobody would escape. Let's look at another example! When a man-made building catches on fire, dozens of people die. When the forest catches on fire, have you ever heard of a tiger burned to death in its own cave?" The tiger laughed so hard that it was out of breath.

"This makes so much sense! Tigers are definitely more advanced. But how about transportation? I haven't heard of tigers driving cars!" the monkey said.

"Humans have weak bodies. They can't run fast, and they can't walk for too long, so they have no choice but to drive. You must know that the cars they drive are not made by the drivers. One car is put together by hundreds of people! If the engine breaks down, they can't drive. If they're out of gasoline, they can't drive. If they don't have a license, they can't drive. If road conditions are terrible, they can't drive. Even when everything works out and they can drive, car accidents happen." The tiger proudly continued, "I bet you've never heard of tigers bumping into other tigers and killing dozens of tigers by accident!"

"Yes! Yes! Yes! Yes! Yes! …" the monkey said yes ten times while nodding dozens of times. At that very moment, a distant gunshot rang out.

"Uh oh! Humans are here! I have to run now!" The tiger disappeared deep into the forest without even waiting to say bye.

"Hey!" the monkey yelled. "Didn't you say that humans are inferior to tigers in every way? Then why are you afraid of them?"

"Because they understand how to look out for each other and work together!" answered the tiger, in a faint distant voice.

天堂雞舍

The Heavenly Chicken Coop

養雞場結束營業，場主夫婦把幾百隻雞
抓走，然後關門離開。就在他們抓雞的時候，
兩隻雞趁亂溜了出去，立刻躲進樹林。看場
主夫婦離開，牠們回到雞場，想進去吃剩下
的糧食，但門關上了，怎麼啄都啄不開。

128

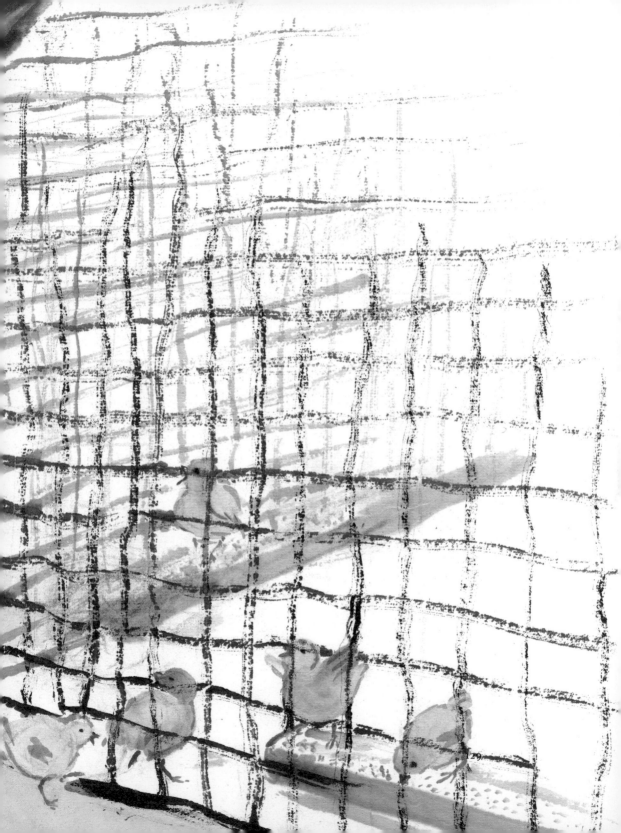

這一公一母兩隻雞只好自己設法覓食，每天從早到晚，東扒扒、西啄啄，勉強吃飽。

　　牠們還生了一窩小雞，看著下一代出世，好開心！因為牠們從小是被孵化器孵出來的，從沒見過爸爸媽媽，不像現在美滿的一家：大公雞、大母雞，還有六隻小雞。

　　牠們教雞娃娃怎麼從草上面啄小小的種子，怎麼在一片砂礫中分辨可吃的東西；還有，昆蟲雖然不好抓，但是眼明嘴快還是啄得到。

　　有一天牠們帶六個雞娃娃去養雞場，繞著那個用鐵絲網圍起來的地方，大公雞介紹：「這是爸爸媽媽以前住的地方，我們完全不必費力覓食，就有吃不完的食物送到眼前，雞舍中間還有泉水湧出，比外面河裡的水都甜。而且養雞場有屋頂，不怕颱風下雨，不像咱們在外面，一下雨就成落湯雞。對了！還有個大好處，是沒有黃鼠狼，不像現在咱們一家總得戰戰兢兢地藏在草叢裡。」

小雞們問：「為什麼不回去呢？」

母雞說：「回不去啦！大門關上了，只能隔著鐵絲網往裡面看，瞧！裡面剩了好多穀子，見得到吃不著！」

「回得去啊！」一隻小雞說。接著就從門邊鐵絲網的縫隙鑽了過去。另外幾隻小雞也立刻跟了進去，齊聲叫雞爸爸和雞媽媽。

公雞母雞低著頭看看鐵絲網，嘆口氣：「爸爸媽媽太大了，鑽不進去，不像你們小，很容易就鑽過去。」

「這裡好大好大喲！」「真的，好多好吃的東西喲！」「一排一排槽子，裡面都有零食吃！」小雞興奮地喊，接著低頭猛吃。

　　眼看天要黑了，雞爸爸雞媽媽喊：「快出來，回家了！」

　　小雞很聽話，都從原路鑽出雞舍。只是不斷問：「為什麼要出來？裡面那麼好，為什麼不讓我們留在裡面？」

　　公雞說：「因為裡面危險！」

　　「危險！」十二隻眼睛盯著爸爸。

　　「因為你們可能進得去、出不來。」母雞接過話回答。

　　「為什麼？」六隻小雞盯著媽媽。

　　「因為你們現在小，一鑽就進去了，等你們身體長大，就鑽不出來了！」

小雞們似懂非懂，第二天又早上鑽進去，傍晚鑽出來。第三天、第四天、第五天都一樣。

　　第六天下起傾盆大雨，小雞怕雨，說裡面既乾又暖，都留在裡面。

　　雨連下了兩個多禮拜，小雞們也就留在雞舍吃吃喝喝快樂度過兩個多禮拜，任雞媽媽雞爸爸怎麼喊都不出來。

　　天晴了，總算有隻小雞想回到爸媽身邊，牠走到鐵絲網，像以前一樣，先把頭探出去，但是接著就卡住了，因為牠的翅膀已經長大，加上吃得胖胖的身子，怎麼擠都擠不出去，還擠掉了一堆毛，好疼啊！

　　「就留在裡面吧！裡面多好？」其他的小雞說：「瞧！還有那麼多食物，雖然是以前幾百隻雞吃剩的，現在咱們六個吃，也一輩子吃不完。」

　　六隻小雞都留了下來，過得快樂極了。就算爸爸媽媽一直呼喚，也不出去。因為牠們要出去也出不去了！

　　六隻小雞都長大了，長得跟爸爸媽媽一樣大。

　　這一天突然大門響。吱一聲！養雞場主夫婦推開門。

　　「天哪！裡面還有這麼多隻，走的那天居然沒看到。」老闆娘說：「幸虧咱們回來看一眼。」

　　接著兩口子把六隻雞逼到角落，兩三下全抓住，扔進後車廂。還一邊抓一邊說：「還挺肥的呢！回去可以燉湯給孩子吃。」

　　車子走遠了。雞爸爸和雞媽媽從樹叢裡走出來，掉下眼淚。

「孩子太笨了！」雞媽媽說。

「其實也不笨。」雞爸爸嘆口氣：「咱們小時候，也能從那個小縫逃出來，咱們為什麼沒逃？咱們不是一樣嗎？以前同住的幾百隻雞不都一樣嗎？」

The chicken farm was closing its business. The husband and wife farm owners snatched up their hundreds of chickens, closed the gate, and departed. Just as they were capturing the chickens, two chickens escaped amidst the chaos and hid in the woods. Seeing that the owners departed, the two chickens returned to the farm. They wanted to eat the leftover food inside, but the gate was closed and would not open again, no matter how much they pecked.

One male and one female, these two chickens had no choice but to try foraging for food. Every day from morning to night, they dug around here and pecked around there, eating barely enough to feel full.

They also hatched a whole nest of baby chicks. Seeing the next generation enter this world, they felt overjoyed! They themselves were hatched from an incubator, so they had never met their parents. Their own childhoods were nothing like the beautiful happy family they had now: big rooster, big hen, and six baby chicks.

They taught the chicks how to peck for tiny seeds on grass and how to determine what's edible on gravel. Also, even though bugs were hard to catch, with clear eyes and a quick beak, it was possible to catch them.

One day, they brought the six chicks to the chicken farm. Walking around that wire-fenced place, the rooster introduced: "This is where Daddy and Mommy used to live. We did not need to work or forage at all; more food than we could ever eat just appeared before our eyes. There was even spring water gushing out in the middle of the chicken coop—water sweeter than the river outside. Also, the farm had a roof, so we were not afraid of wind or rain—unlike now, living outside, looking like we fell in soup whenever it rains. Oh yes! Another great benefit was the lack of weasels, so we didn't have to tremble and hide in the tall grass like we always do now."

The chicks asked, "Why don't we go back?"

The hen replied, "We can't go back! The gate has closed. We can only peer in through the wire fence. Look! There is so much millet left inside. We see it but can't eat it!"

"We can go back!" said a chick, as he slipped through a gap in the wire fence by the gate. The other chicks immediately followed, and they called for Daddy Chicken and Mommy

Chicken in unison.

The rooster and the hen lowered their heads to look at the wire fence. They sighed and said, "Daddy and Mommy are too big to slip in. We're not like you little ones, who can slip through easily."

"This place is really really big!" "For real, there is so much yummy food!" "There are rows and rows of slots, all with snacks inside!" The chicks excitedly shouted and then went on an eating binge.

Seeing that the skies were darkening, Daddy Chicken and Mommy Chicken shouted, "Hurry back! Time to go home!"

The chicks were very obedient, and they all slipped back out through the same gap. However, they repeatedly asked, "Why did we have to come out? It's so nice inside. Why couldn't you let us stay inside?"

The rooster said, "Because it's dangerous inside!"

"Dangerous!" Twelve eyes stared at Daddy.

"Because maybe you can get in but cannot get out," the hen took over and replied.

"Why?" The six chicks stared at Mommy.

"Because you're small now and can slip right through. When your bodies grow bigger, you won't be able to slip out anymore!"

The chicks seemed to somewhat understand. The next day, again they entered in the morning and slipped out in the evening. The third day, the fourth day, and the fifth day were the same.

On the sixth day, a torrential rainstorm began. The chicks were afraid of rain. They said since it was dry and warm inside, they would stay inside.

The rain continued for more than two weeks. The chicks also stayed in the chicken coop for more than two weeks, happily eating and drinking. No matter how much Mommy Chicken and Daddy Chicken shouted, they would not come out.

The skies cleared. Finally, one chick wanted to go back to his parents. He walked to the wire fence, and just like before, he first poked his head through. But then he was stuck. His wings had already grown bigger, and his body was fat from eating. He squeezed and squeezed but still could not squeeze through. He squeezed off some feathers though—that hurt!

"Let's just stay inside! Isn't it nice in here?" said the other chicks. "Look! There's still so much food. Even though these are leftovers from the hundreds of chickens before, now for the six of us, it's more than enough to last our whole lives."

All six chicks stayed behind, and they lived extremely happily. Although Daddy and Mommy kept calling, they did not leave—because even if they wanted to, they could not leave!

The six chicks grew up. They grew as big as Daddy and Mommy.

On this day, there was suddenly a sound at the gate. Squeak! The husband and wife farm owners opened the gate.

"Oh my! There are still so many inside. We apparently did not see them the day we left," said the wife. "Thank goodness we came back for another look."

Then, the couple forced the six chickens into a corner, captured them all in a matter of seconds, and threw them into the trunk. They even said as they were capturing: "Hey, they're quite plump! We can make soup for the kids when we get back."

The car drove away. Daddy Chicken and Mommy Chicken walked out from the bushes, and they wept.

"The kids were too stupid!" said Mommy Chicken.

"Actually, they were not stupid," said Daddy Chicken with a sigh. "When we were little, we could have escaped from that small gap too, but why didn't we escape? Weren't we the same? And weren't our hundreds of roommates the same too?"

鞋子們的討論會

The Symposium of the Shoes

　　有天晚上，櫃子裡的皮鞋們舉行了一場討論會。

　　為了敬老，首先由一雙彎腰駝背、滿臉皺紋，而且牙齒漏風的皮鞋老爹發言，他顫抖地說：

　　「我覺得人們是最沒良心的，因為世界上任何動物都用他們自己的腳板走路，只有人類狠毒地剝下動物的皮，做成皮鞋穿，不管太陽晒得柏油路面冒泡或是雨水混合著泥漿；也無論地上有又尖又硬的石頭或刺人的荊棘，他們都毫不憐惜地踩著我們亂走，要我們為他們受苦受難，好讓他們的腳能又白又嫩。而且，當我們破損變形不堪再穿的時候，他們就把我們往垃圾桶裡一扔，甚至還怕把手弄髒，而急著去洗手。他們不念主僕的情分，不念我們的功勞苦勞，連把我們甩掉之後，還要侮辱我們，你說人類可恨不可恨？」說到這兒，皮鞋老爹又氣又累地乾咳不止，咳出不少沙子。

這時坐在櫃子最上方，剛加入鞋櫃不久的皮鞋小夥子開口了：

「皮鞋老爹太誇張了！他一定是因為年紀太大，而且牙痛，所以喪失記憶、亂罵主人。我覺得人類是最有良心、最體貼，且能以德報怨的。」

所有的皮鞋都露出懷疑的眼光。

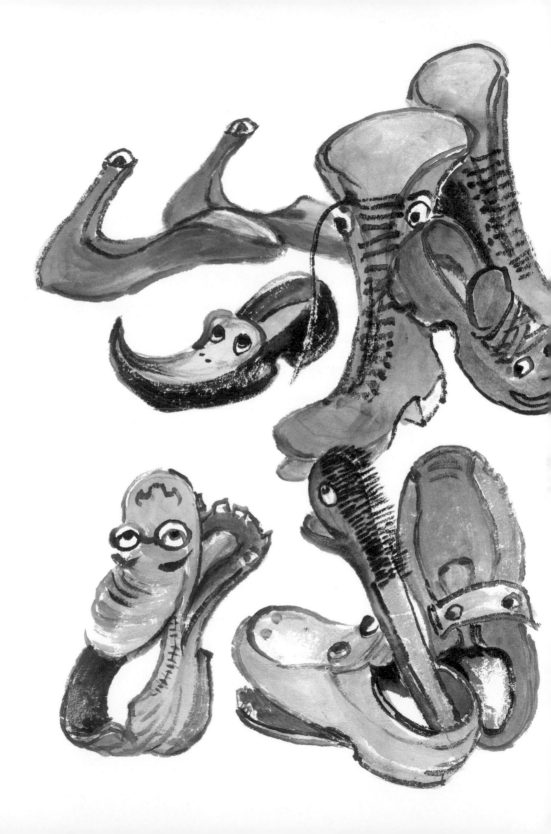

「至少我覺得主人對我就相當好。」新皮鞋小
夥子繼續滔滔不絕地說：「他每天擦拭我，使我
一塵不染；他每週為我刷上鞋油，使我總是神采
煥發；他甚至走路都特別小心，乘公共汽車更不
時閃躲別人的腳步，唯恐我受絲毫的損傷。至於
陰天下雨、長途跋涉，他從不要我出馬，而留我
在家睡覺，這是多麼體貼啊！尤其不簡單的是，
他以德報怨的胸襟；儘管我因為年輕氣盛，有時
咬他幾口，害他腳跟起泡，他還是對我滿臉笑容，
並時時在人前誇讚我的身價。他真是偉大、慈祥，
而且⋯⋯」

　　「夠了！夠了！你們都太偏激了！讓我來講幾
句公道話。」已經開始發福的中年鞋子打斷小夥

子的話：「我記得主人起初確實是那麼慈祥體貼，但是漸漸地他就露出喜新厭舊的本性，先是不再每天給我搽面霜，後來連臉都不為我擦了。而且過去別人如果踩我一腳，他一定會瞪上那人老半天，然後掏出潔白的手帕，彎下腰，輕輕為我擦去淚水；但是如今，別人踩我好幾下，他都不在乎，還穿著我去爬山和踢足球。」說到這兒，他長長地嘆口氣，低頭看看滿身的泥土，搖著頭說：

「為了他，我真是犧牲太大了。他的腳長得怪，我特別扭著腰、伸長脖子、挺著肚子去適應他，使他穿著舒服。豈知，就因為如此，舉凡粗重的工作、長遠的跋涉，他必定要我出馬；為此我擦傷了漂亮的臉頰，跌落了整齊的牙齒，不但沒獲得報償，他反而因我失去美貌，任何宴會大典都不再帶我去了。所幸他偶爾還會拍拍我，對他太太說我是最舒服的鞋子。並在他心情好時，為我搽上一點面霜，使我的怨氣能稍稍平息。」

　　最後，站在一旁老半天的鞋刷也開口了：「我覺得你們根本不必爭辯，人類不單對鞋子，他們對任何東西都這樣；像我，先是被用來刷帽子，而後刷衣服，現在則刷鞋子，只怕明天也要進垃圾桶了。有用的時候說你好，並給你重任；沒用的時候，頭也不回地把你甩掉，這大概是人類的本性吧？幸虧他們對同類不至如此，當父母年老無用時，他們還知道孝敬；當妻子人老珠黃時，他們還知道體貼；當朋友窮愁潦倒時，他們還知道濟助。就憑這一點，他們還算得上是人，如果有一天，他們對親友都失去了情義，就連我們鞋子、刷子也不如了。」

　　全體鞋子都熱烈鼓掌，使得櫃子裡塵土飛揚。
　　「謝了！謝了！請別再鼓掌。」鞋刷大聲喊著：「否則要為你們刷洗，我又有得忙了。」

One night, the shoes in the cabinet held a symposium.

Out of respect for elders, they let a pair of old grandpa shoes speak first. With his back hunched, face full of wrinkles, and teeth leaking air, he said in a trembling voice:

"I think humans are the most heartless. All the other animals in the world use their own feet to walk. Only humans viciously skin animals to make leather shoes. Regardless of whether the asphalt pavement is bubbling under the hot sun, regardless of whether there are sharp and hard rocks or spiky thorns on the ground, humans unpityingly step on us as they walk all over the place. They make us suffer on their behalf, so that their feet stay pale and tender. Moreover, when we become too damaged and deformed for them to wear, they just toss us into the trash can and even wash their hands right afterward, in fear of our dirtiness. They give no thought to the bond between master and servant, no thought to our hard work.

Even after they throw us away, they insult us. Wouldn't you say humans are incredibly hateful?" Pausing here, the pair of grandpa shoes coughed repeatedly from both anger and exhaustion. He coughed up quite a bit of sand.

◉

At this time, sitting at the very top of the cabinet, a pair of young lad shoes who recently joined the cabinet spoke up:

"Grandpa Shoes exaggerates too much! It must be because he's old and his teeth hurt, so he's losing his memory and complaining about Master. I think humans are the most kind and caring, and they're virtuous even when wronged."

All the other shoes looked at him suspiciously.

"At least I think Master treats me quite well." The new pair of young lad shoes continued without stopping: "He wipes me clean every day, so that there's not a single speck of dust on me. He brushes shoeshine on me every week, so that I'm always glowing. He even walks especially carefully; when riding buses, he frequently dodges other people's steps, for fear that I suffer any injury. On rainy days and for long treks, he never makes me go on duty and instead lets me sleep at home. How caring he is! The most amazing thing is his unwavering virtue in the face of wrongdoing. Since I'm young and vigorous, I bite him sometimes, which gives him blisters on his heels. But he still smiles at me and always praises my worth in front of other people. He is truly great, benevolent, and…"

◉

"Enough! Enough! You are all too extreme! Let me speak some justice." A pair of middle-aged shoes with a chubby belly interrupted the young lad: "I remember when Master was truly that benevolent and caring in the beginning, but he gradually exposed his nature of liking the new and despising the old. First, he stopped applying face lotion on me every day; later, he even stopped wiping my face. Also, in the past, whenever someone stepped on me, he would glare at that person for a long time, then take out a perfectly clean handkerchief, bend down, and gently wipe away my tears. But now, people can step on me multiple times, and he doesn't seem to care. He even wears me to climb mountains and play soccer." Pausing here, he let out a long sigh, looked down at his dirt-covered body, and shook his head as he continued:

"For him, I have truly sacrificed too much. His feet are shaped oddly, so I purposely bent my back, elongated my neck, and pushed out my belly to accommodate him and help him feel comfortable. But who could have known, precisely because I do that, he always makes me go on duty for the toughest jobs and the longest treks. That's how I bruised my beautiful face and broke my neat teeth. Not only did he never reward me, but rather he stopped taking me to banquets and ceremonies because I lost my good looks. Luckily, from time to time, he still pats me affectionately and tells his wife that I am his most comfortable pair of shoes. And when he's in a good mood, he applies some face lotion on me, and then my resentment subsides for a little while."

◉

Finally, the shoe brush who had been standing nearby for a long time spoke up too: "I think you all have no reason to argue. Humans don't just treat shoes this way; they treat all things this way. Take me for example. I was first used to brush hats, then to brush clothes, and now to brush shoes. Maybe tomorrow I'll be in the trash can. When you're useful, they praise you and give you important responsibilities. When you're no longer useful, they throw you away without looking back. I suppose this is human nature? Fortunately, they don't treat their own kind this way. When their parents are elderly and useless, they still know to respect. When their wives are old and unattractive, they still know to be considerate. When their friends fall on hard times, they still know to help. Just based on this point, they're still worthy of being called humans. If one day they lose affection for even their family and friends, then they would be worse than shoes and brushes."

All the shoes gave such a warm round of applause that dust flew about the cabinet.

"Thank you! Thank you! Please stop applauding," the shoe brush shouted. "Or else to brush and clean you, I'll be busy again."

傳家寶

The Family Heirloom

家道中落的父親，臨終，把獨子叫到牀前，指指牀下，顫抖著說：

　　「這兒有一卷畫，是唐代王維的真跡，你爺爺留下來的。」苦笑了一下：「這麼多年來，家裡的錢被人坑的坑、倒的倒，可是我始終守著這卷畫。我心裡很踏實。我自己告訴自己，我還有路，真絕了，還能把這卷畫賣了。就這樣，我居然撐下來了，能把這幅畫，好好交到你手裡。」

　　話說完，老人就嚥了氣。

　　喪事辦完，兒子在老母的陪同下，拉出牀下的鐵箱子，打開來，果然有一幅精裱的古畫，象牙的軸頭，織錦的卷首；展開來，雖然絹色早已變暗，但是筆力蒼勁，一看就是幅傳世的無價之寶。

　　「把畫賣了吧！」老母說：「好供你去留學。」

「不！」兒子說：「不能賣，以前家裡那麼苦，爸爸都撐下來，沒賣，我也能撐下來，除非路走絕了⋯⋯」

天無絕人之路。兒子居然靠為人補習、出國打工和得到的獎學金，順利地修到了學位，還交到了一個可愛的女朋友。

「你有多少錢？能娶我的女兒？」女朋友的父親不太看得上這個窮小子。

年輕人一笑，說：「伯父，我家窮，但也不窮。說實話我們還挺有錢，因為我家傳下來一卷唐代王維的真跡，只是我媽不願賣，賣了最少能買一幢房子。下次我拿來，您看看就知道了。」

女朋友的父親笑笑：「不用看了！瞧你說話的

樣子，就知道不假。我佩服你，那麼苦，還能守住那幅畫；我也相信，你能守住我女兒。」

他們結婚了，胼手胝足，打下一片江山；二十年後，成為大企業家。

他們有兩個兒子，也都各有所成。每年春節，作父親的都會在拈香拜祖先之後，再去把手洗乾淨，在老妻的協助下，打開那張傳家之寶：

「瞧瞧！你們爺爺留下來的寶貝，『詩中有畫，畫中有詩』，王維的畫，爺爺早年經商失敗，又被人騙，一窮二白的時候，明明把畫賣了，就能過好日子，但是他咬著牙，硬是不賣。」老人笑笑：「爸爸也一樣，明明賣了畫，就有了留學的錢，可也捨不得，靠自己撐下來了。也幸虧如此，拿這幅畫，贏得你外公的青睞，娶到你們的媽媽。

將來這卷畫就傳給你們，希望你們也能好好守著。」

　　兩夫婦都死了。畫從保險箱裡拿出來。兄弟二人搶著要，甚至翻了臉。

　　「得了！」作哥哥的一拍桌子：「把它賣掉算了，畫不好分，錢好分，一人一半。」

　　這幅唐代王維的神品山水畫，終於被兩兄弟送到拍賣公司。收藏界早聽說有這麼一卷畫，也早派人出來打聽底價。

　　只是，拍賣目錄印出來，居然沒有那幅畫。據說兩兄弟又後悔了，抽回那幅王維真跡。

　　而且兩人顯然取得諒解，古畫歸給老大；為這事，老二的太太還很不高興，覺得丈夫無能。

直到丈夫在她耳邊輕輕說了幾句話，又拿出拍賣公司的鑑定書，太太才笑了。

　　又過幾十年，老大也將逝了。

　　臨終，他把孩子叫到牀前，如同他爺爺當年把他爸爸喊到牀前一般，顫抖著說：

　　「咱們銀行保險箱裡，藏著一卷傳家之寶。你的曾祖父靠它支撐著，熬過難關；你的祖父又靠它撐著，克服萬難；我又和你叔叔，從畫裡得到很多教訓，彼此關照著過一生。而今，這畫傳給你了。困苦的時候常想想你有這個寶，你就不會自嘆不如人。但是，記住！你絕對不能賣了這幅畫……」

There was a family that was once rich but now poor. On his deathbed, the father called his only son to his side. He pointed beneath the bed, and in a trembling voice, he spoke:

"Under here is a painting, an authentic masterpiece by Wang Wei of the Tang Dynasty. Your grandfather left it to me." He forced a smile. "Over the years, our family's money has been swindled away and lost, but I always held onto this painting. My heart was at ease. I told myself I still had hope. I knew that if I were truly destitute, then I could sell this painting. Just like that, I survived the hard times, and now I am able to place this painting into your hands."

The old man finished speaking and took his last breath.

After the funeral, the son and his elderly mother moved the metal box out from under the bed. Inside was an exquisite old painting, mounted on a scroll made of ivory and embroidered silk. They saw that although the painting had darkened with age, the brushwork was still bold and lively. It was clearly a priceless treasure passed down through many generations.

"Let's sell the painting!" said the elderly mother. "It will pay for your education."

"No!" said the son. "We cannot sell it. Our family was even poorer in the past, and Father survived those hard times without selling. I can survive too. We will not sell, unless we become truly hopeless…"

◉

There is always a road to hope. With the money he made from tutoring and other jobs, and with the help of a scholarship, the son was able to finish school. He even had an adorable girlfriend.

"How much money do you have? You think you can marry my daughter?" The girlfriend's father did not think much of this poor young man.

The young man smiled and said, "Sir, my family may be poor, but we are also not really poor. We are actually quite wealthy because we have a family heirloom, an authentic masterpiece by Wang Wei of the Tang Dynasty. My mother refuses to sell it, but if we were to sell it, we could buy a house for sure. I'll bring it next time, and you'll believe me when you see it."

The girlfriend's father smiled. "I don't need to see it! Just by seeing the way you talk, I know it's true. I admire you for holding onto that painting, even while living in poverty. I also believe that you can hold onto my daughter."

They got married. They worked hard together and achieved greatness everywhere they went. Twenty years later, they were known as successful entrepreneurs.

They had two sons, who were both accomplished in their own ways. Every Chinese New Year, the father would burn incense and pray to ancestors, and then after washing his hands and with the help of his wife, he would take out that treasured painting:

"Look! Your grandfather left this treasure to us. There is scenery within the poetry, and there is poetry within the painting—the work of Wang Wei. Grandfather's business failed when he was young, and he lost the rest of his money to conmen. When he was living in poverty, he could have sold this painting to live a nice life; but he pushed through the hard times and insisted on not selling." The old man smiled. "I was the same. I could have sold the painting to pay for school, but I could not let it go. I survived on my own. And thank goodness, the fact that I kept this painting helped me win your maternal grandfather's favor to let me marry your mother. In the future, this painting will be passed onto the two of you. I hope you can also hold onto it."

⊙

Both the husband and the wife passed away. The painting was taken out of the safety deposit box. The two brothers fought over who would get it, and emotions were at fever pitch.

"Fine!" said the older brother as he slammed the table. "Let's just sell it! We can't split the painting, but we can split the money, 50/50."

This Tang Dynasty landscape painting by Wang Wei was consigned to an auction house by the two brothers. Collectors had heard since long ago that such a painting existed, and they sent associates to find out the estimated price.

However, when the auction catalogue was released, it did not include this painting. Supposedly, the brothers regretted their decision and took the painting back.

Moreover, the two men seemed to forgive each other and arrive at a consensus: the older brother would keep the painting. Because of this, the younger brother's wife was extremely upset and thought her husband was useless.

Her husband whispered something in her ear and showed her the auction house's authentication report. That's when the wife finally smiled.

A few decades later, the older brother was nearing the end of his life.

On his deathbed, he called his child over, just like how his grandfather had called his father over. He spoke in a trembling voice:

"In our safety deposit box at the bank, there is a family heirloom. Your great-grandfather held onto hope because of it and survived hard times. Your grandfather also held onto hope because of it and surmounted numerous obstacles. Your uncle and I learned many lessons because of this painting, and we've looked after each other our whole lives. Today, this painting is passed onto you. In difficult times, think about how you have this treasure, and you will never feel sorry for yourself. But remember! You must never sell this painting..."

橡樹與小草

●

The Oak Tree and the Grass

在一處人跡罕見的曠野，有一條老鐵道；由
於火車很少通過，所以不但鐵道兩旁，連鐵軌之
間也長滿了小草。到溫暖的季節，小草們織成一
大片綠色的地毯，把鐵道也給掩沒了，只有每個
月唯一一班火車通過的時候，才讓人們想起：原
來這兒還有一條鐵道。

某日，當火車又疾駛而過，小草們都低頭行
禮時，有一粒橡樹的種子，從車上滑落，正掉在
兩軌之間。

「這是什麼啊？」最先抬起頭的小草驚訝地叫。

「好像是顆種子。」所有的小草都伸長了脖子湊過來看：「但是為什麼這麼大？好像有我們種子的幾百倍呢！」

「各位好！」橡樹子從昏迷中醒轉，環視四周的小草，高興地打招呼，並自我介紹：「我是一顆橡樹子。」

「橡樹？」所有的小草都面面相覷：「我們從來沒聽說過啊！」

「我們這裡沒有樹，只有草，我們世世代代生長在這兒，從來沒見過一棵樹，因為這裡冬天特別冷，風又大，不適合樹的生長。」一株比較年長的草神情嚴肅地說：「我看，你還是快回到你來的地方去吧！」

「我已經來了，怎麼回得去呢？」橡樹子皺著眉說，但是跟著環顧四周，又笑了：「這裡多好啊！我喜歡這裡，我不怕狂風和霜雪，決定在這兒生根，長成一棵高大的橡樹……」

「好！」沒等他說完，四周成千上萬的小草，就發出一陣歡呼：「我們喜歡你，我們需要一棵高大的樹，我們要你來領導。」

於是橡樹子在這兒生了根、發了芽。起初他長得很慢，小草們由春天萌發，不到盛夏就能長到一尺高，所以夾在草叢中，除了葉子比較大些，小橡樹並不怎麼突出；當每個月火車開來的時候，小橡樹也和小草們一樣，早早就彎下腰，讓那龐然大物從頭上飛馳而過。

但是到了暮秋，小草們都逐漸凋萎枯黃的時

候，橡樹雖然也落了葉子，仍然直直地站在那兒。當火車開來，由於沒有小草們的簇擁，橡樹反而站得更直了，所幸火車除了前面保險槓會把橡樹撞得一個跟蹌，車子的底盤倒不會傷害他。所以當冬天過去，小草們又復甦的時候，都訝異小橡樹仍然站在那兒。

「我爸爸有四十尺高，他的頭經常遮在雲裡，他一伸手，就能摘下天上的星星。」小橡樹總是得意地對小草們說。每次講到這兒，小草們都會仰起頭，把嘴張得好大好大，羨慕極了：「我們多高興你能在這兒生根啊！」小草們說：「當你長到像你爸爸一樣高時，我們就可以聽你訴說天空的一切了！」

「我也會抓幾顆星星給你們。」小橡樹臉上泛著光彩。

　　但是小橡樹也有他的煩惱，就是每個月火車通過時，小草們都一低頭就過了，他卻難免損傷幾片葉子，有時還會折到腰，而且這種情況愈來愈嚴重。

　　「你為什麼不把腰彎低一點呢？再不然，乾脆躺在地上算了，等火車過了之後再站起來，何必跟火車去爭呢？」小草們都這樣勸他。

　　小橡樹何嘗不知道，可是他的身體硬，怎麼也不可能躺下來，眼看情況愈來愈糟，他真希望自己不再長了，甚至縮小幾分，跟小草們一樣不是就夠了嗎？但在轉念之間，他又想：「為什麼我不趕快長大長高呢？如果我長成幾人合抱的大樹，火車也得讓著我。」

於是當小橡樹折損小枝子，就趕快伸出另一條新枝；當火車刮去了他的葉子，就趕快長新的葉芽。但是每當火車呼嘯而去，小草們紛紛披倒，再站起的時候，小橡樹又是遍體鱗傷。

當然把握沒有火車通過的一個月時間，小橡
樹又恢復了光彩，只是他發現自己的腰愈來愈硬，
連弓身都有困難了。

　　終於有一天，當火車又轟隆轟隆地遠去之後，
小草們發現小橡樹已經被連根扯斷。

　　「你為什麼不能跟我們一樣彎腰屈膝？」小草
們傷心地哭著，看著小橡樹的屍體變為枯枝，被
風吹走。

　　鐵軌間、鐵道邊、鐵道的四周，仍然是一片
青青的草原，火車不通過的日子，這裡真是無比
寧靜祥和，只偶爾聽到小草們喁喁私語：「作一
株平凡的小草，是多麼快樂的事！」

In a wilderness where human sightings were rare, there was an old railroad. Since the train passed through very infrequently, small grasses grew not only on both sides of the track but also between the rails. When the seasons turned warm, the grasses weaved together into a big green carpet that covered over the railroad. Only once a month, when the one scheduled train passed through, did anyone remember: there is still a railroad here.

One day, when the train quickly passed by again, when the grasses bowed their heads in salutation, an acorn slipped off the train and landed right in the middle of the track.

"What is this?" the first grass that raised its head screamed in surprise.

"It looks like a seed." All the grasses craned their necks to get a view. "But why is it so big? It looks hundreds of times bigger than our seeds!"

"Hello, everybody!" The acorn woke up from its daze, looked around at the small grasses, happily greeted everyone, and introduced itself: "I am an acorn, the seed of an oak tree."

"An oak tree?" All the grasses looked at each other. "We have not heard of it before!"

"There are no trees here; there is only grass. We have lived here for many generations without ever seeing a tree because winters are especially cold here, and the winds are strong. It is not a suitable place for trees to grow," an older blade of grass said, with a stern face. "I think you should quickly go back to where you came from!"

"I have already arrived. How can I go back?" the acorn said with a frown. But then it looked around at its surroundings and smiled again. "How nice it is here! I like it here. I am not afraid of fierce winds and frosty snow. I have decided to take root here, and I will grow into a tall oak tree…"

"Okay!" Before the acorn could finish, the tens of thousands of grasses let out a cheer: "We like you. We need a tall tree. We want you to lead us."

Therefore, the acorn took root and sprouted into a seedling. At first, it grew very slowly. Since the grasses germinated in spring and grew a foot tall by mid-summer, the little oak tree lived among the grasses and did not stand out much, besides having slightly larger leaves. When the train came every month, the little oak tree did as the small grasses did; they bent over ahead of time and let that monstrous thing fly over their heads.

But by late autumn, when the grasses gradually withered and yellowed, although the oak tree also lost its leaves, it still stood there upright. When the train came, without the grasses crowding around, the oak tree actually stood even straighter. Fortunately, only the train's bumper hit the oak tree and made it stagger; the train bogie did not injure it. After winter passed and the grasses were revived, they were all surprised to see the little oak tree still standing there.

"My father is 40 feet tall. His head is often hidden in the clouds. He can reach up and pick a star out of the sky," the little oak tree always proudly said to the small grasses. Every time it got to that part, the grasses would lift their faces up and open their mouths wide in admiration. "We are so happy that you could take root here!" the grasses said. "When you grow to be as tall as your father, then we can hear you tell stories about the sky!"

"I'll also capture a few stars for you," said the little oak tree, glowing with joy.

However, the little oak tree had its own troubles. Every month when the train came, the small grasses just had to bow their heads and let it pass, but the oak tree would inevitably lose some leaves and sometimes even twist its back. And this situation was getting worse.

"Why don't you bend a bit lower? Otherwise, you can just lie down and wait for the train to pass, and then stand back up. Why fight against the train?" the grasses advised.

The little oak tree knew these things, but its body was stiff. It was impossible for it to lie down. Sensing the worsening situation, it wished it would stop growing or, better yet, shrink a few inches. Wouldn't it be enough to look the same as the small grasses? But then, it changed its mind and thought, "Why don't I hurry and grow big and grow tall? If I become a magnificent tree, then the train would have to yield to me."

Therefore, every time the little oak tree broke a branch, it would quickly extend a new branch. Every time the train shaved off its leaves, it would quickly grow new leaves. But every time the train whizzed by, after the small grasses fell over one by one and then stood up again, the little oak tree would be covered in bruises.

Of course, it seized the moments between each month's train and recovered to full glory. However, it noticed that its waist was increasingly stiff. Even bending became difficult.

Finally, one day, after the train thunderously faded into the distance, the small grasses noticed that the little oak tree had become broken and uprooted.

"Why didn't you bend and kneel like we did?" the grasses sorrowfully cried, as they watched the little oak tree's body transform into dry branches and blow away in the wind.

Between the rails, by the track, and all around, it is still a green meadow. On the days without a train, this place is incomparably peaceful and serene—except occasionally, one can hear small grasses whispering: "To be a plain blade of grass is such a happy thing!"

185

散盡家財
的大楓樹

The Maple Tree that
Gave Away Everything

楓樹對上帝抱怨：

「春天，我拚命擠出嫩芽，給小鳥當蔬菜吃。

夏天，我拚命長出大葉，給小動物當陽傘遮蔭。

秋天，我打扮得豔麗如火，給人們美的饗宴。

我現在還能做什麼呢？」

上帝說：「既然你什麼都有過了，就洗盡鉛華，回歸平淡吧！」

楓樹實在捨不得放棄一切，但是候鳥南飛了，小動物冬眠了，人們回家過年了！自己好像抱著大把鈔票的財主，手上滿滿，心裡空空。

「好吧！我捨！」楓樹終於想通，一揮手，把葉子全部捐給大地，舉起空空的手對天喊：「我一無所有了！」

天沒說話，但是撒下白花花的銀子……

The maple tree complained to God: "In spring, I squeezed with all my might to sprout new leaves, for little birds to eat as vegetables. In summer, I grew with all my might to form big leaves, for little animals to use as parasols. In autumn, I dressed up to look as glamorous as fire, for humans to take delight in the beauty. What can I still do now?"

God said, "Since you've already had everything, then wash away all splendor and return to simplicity!"

The maple tree felt deeply reluctant to give up everything, but the migratory birds had flown south, the little animals had entered hibernation, and the humans had gone home for the holidays! The maple tree felt like a rich person holding a pile of money—full hands, empty heart.

"Okay! I'll let go!" The maple tree finally came round. With a wave, it donated all its leaves to the earth. It raised its empty hands to the sky and shouted, "Now I have nothing!"

God did not speak, but white shimmering silver sprinkled down from the sky…

國家圖書館出版品預行編目（CIP）資料

我們靠自己 We rely on ourselves
／劉墉 中文、圖；劉倚帆 英文
-- 初版 . -- 新北市：遠足文化 , 2020.10
面 ；公分
ISBN　978-986-508-075-4（平裝）
1. 修身　　2. 寓言
192 . 1　　　　　109014105

遠　足　心　靈

我們
靠自己

We Rely on
Ourselves

中文‧圖 —— 劉墉
英　　文 —— 劉倚帆
監　　製 —— 劉軒
編　　輯 —— 王育涵
總 編 輯 —— 李進文
執 行 長 —— 陳蕙慧

行銷總監 —— 陳雅雯
行銷企劃 —— 尹子麟、張宜倩
視覺設計 —— 江孟達工作室

出 版 者 —— 遠足文化事業股份有限公司 (讀書共和國出版集團)
　　　　　　231 新北市新店區民權路 108-2 號 9 樓
　　　　　　電話 (02) 2218-1417　　傳真 (02) 2218-0727
　　　　　　客服信箱　service@bookrep.com.tw
　　　　　　郵撥帳號　19504465
　　　　　　客服專線　0800-221-029
　　　　　　網　　址　https://www.bookrep.com.tw
　　　　　　臉書專頁　https://www.facebook.com/WalkersCulturalNo.1
　　　　　　法律顧問　華洋法律事務所　蘇文生律師
　　　　　　印　　製　呈靖彩藝有限公司

定　　價 —— 新台幣 330 元
初版一刷 —— 西元 2020 年 10 月
初版三刷 —— 西元 2023 年 10 月
Printed in Taiwan